Library of
Davidson College

THE SIGNS AMONG US
AND OTHER POEMS

*First published 1968
by Routledge & Kegan Paul Ltd.
Broadway House, 68–74 Carter Lane
London, E.C.4*

*Printed in Great Britain
by Cox & Wyman Ltd.
London, Fakenham and Reading*

© *W. W. Robson 1968*

*No part of this book may be reproduced
in any form without permission from
the publisher, except for the quotation
of brief passages in criticism*

SBN 7100 6057 2

W. W. ROBSON

The Signs Among Us
and other poems

Routledge and Kegan Paul
LONDON

CONTENTS

Acknowledgements   *page* ix

I

The Owl's Nest	3
Noonday	4
Questions: Assertions	5
Bluefeather	6
Temporary Standstill	7
The Madness of Lester	8
The Pool of the Ring	10
The Picture Book	11
Waiting	13
Serious Operation	14
The Dispossessed	15
The Others	16
After the Party	17
The Fire Hunt	18
The Silver Tray	20
Brothers	21
Mere Interlude	22
Renewal	24
Tenebrae	25
Thematic Apperception	28

II

The Pretender	31
An Author	33
Murderers of Memory	34
A Hero	35
Lost Laughter of Infancy	36
Mrs. Barberon	39

III

Mysteriarch	45
Three Poems of a Prophetess	46
Perpetual Dancers	48
A Supplication	49
Night	50
Defeat: Oracular	51
Victory	52
Funeral of a Religious	53
Four Pictures in a Gallery	54
Fruit	57
Carnival	58
The Signs Among Us	61
Snows have Gone: Archaic	62
Pavane for Garcés	64
Merciless Riders	66
Water	67
Doldrums	68
Panther's Eyes	69
Reed	70
Fomes Peccati	71
Legend	72
Receding	73
Atonement	74
Alantris	75

Wrestler	76
In March	77
Panther	78
Recovery	79
Demythologizing	80
Metamorphoses	81

ACKNOWLEDGEMENTS

The author and publisher wish to express their thanks to the Editor of *The Observer*, for permission to reprint 'The Owl's Nest', 'The Silver Tray' and 'The Picture Book'.

I

THE OWL'S NEST

We looked for the owl's nest,
Bits of old string and wire
Ruinous, high
In the tormented tower,
Whence amid dark and dirt
Enormous eyes looked out.

Far below us Michael,
Small as a fly, moved on
The old accustomed road
Into the setting sun,
Into the tree-lined west:
We climbed for the owl's nest.

Ruin and desolate height
Had drawn us through the dark.
Humanity was distant,
We pursued the work,
Did not meet those wise
Day-changing glimmering eyes.

NOONDAY

A child frightened in the churchyard,
Menaced by the yew tree,
Menaced by the spire at nightfall,
My father took my hand, quieted my fears,
Showed me the Northern Lights,
The dazzling streamers, the triumphant conflict.
Night became day, remained day.

Many years after, the day darkened round me:
Looking up from the belfry,
The strong light suddenly withdrawn,
I wavered amid an incoherent cloud-assembly,
Inferred a president of shadows.

Until the sun came out at last
Over the yew and spire, and my mind
Joyfully, swiftly, meaningfully spanned
The future and the past:
At noonday.

QUESTIONS: ASSERTIONS

I have said enough about moonlight,
Mock me no more.
Question me, polymaths:
How is it that the soul informs the body?
How is it goodness shines from one man's face,
Evil jumps out of another's?

(Pattern of a snow crystal
The same today as when the first snows fell?)

What have you left me but
Complaints upon the subtleties of nature,
The secret recesses of truth,
The obscurity of things,
The infirmity of man's discerning power?

Let me declare form, surface, current,
The ultimate admonishers.
Let me be light in light,
Speak from the heart of cedars:
Speak with the voice of ancient pines.

BLUEFEATHER

Bluefeather up at dawn:
It took five yards to reach that hill,
It took five years to climb that hill!
The trees
Dandle the morning's childhood in their arms.

Bluefeather by the waterfall,
Impatient for the broad strong face
That through the embittered water-smoke
Lightened the place
With possibilities of day.

(And after him,
In heavy-breathed anxiety,
In awkward piety,
A larger clamberer not yet hopeful of
The clear-eyed ruler of the cloudy hill.)

Bluefeather at the top:
With a brief smile of tenderness and reproach
And rich intensity of expectation.

TEMPORARY STANDSTILL

That old and jealous one
We were rid of long since
Tonight came into my mind,
And I looked up, but at once
His stooping shadow had gone,
Receded from the blind
As quickly as it had come:
And the clock's whirring chime,
The clapper of the bell,
The motions of the will,
Stopped still for me: struck dumb
At the surprises of time.

THE MADNESS OF LESTER

Were you pursued as I was pursued
Did you bend shake bleed like the rowan
Death-rattle like the pine
Burn greyly like the ash
Gall like the oak
Did you awaken as I awoke
Not crying out when struck
Crying when no blow fell
Have you stood as I stood
Not awakening when all awoke

Rowans bow ferny foliage, bleed in scarlet apples, mutter
Sleep sleep
Dead antlers of pine crackle, mutter
You shall not sleep tonight
Pewter-grey ash-stems wither into dryness, mutter
Sleep sleep
Furrowed oaks in agony of wasp-galled trunks, mutter
You shall not sleep tonight

What are these arms that reach out from the trees
These forms that keep
Terribly awake in me the terrible abstracts
Why were they left
What is left to me
Sleep nothing but sleep

Either the forms fade, burn black, blow woodward, blow back
The long-loved leaves, recent remembered riches, or turn track
Furies: heart beating
Where juice runs rich, bad weeds long, lush, the imprecise, the
 broken
Words there; the last, least question stilled, suggestion stilled, the
 spoken the unspoken;
Furies were speaking
Vacuous and inoperative, waking this
Madness at my own images.

You will not cry
What I cry proclaiming that light
Light from decay.
That light white light
Eludes the opposite, since October
Came firing ferny foliage lightly lightly
The wood over the world over the shaking sleepers the summer
 over
Themselves the dancing lights lightening my sleep at nights
They cry hoarsely as I cry turn crying as I cry
Turn crying as you dare not cry
Maddened by their own images, rather than turn death-black,
 turn back,
Or stay, decay, putrescence shining, light, the unblest light.
How shall I sleep tonight?

THE POOL OF THE RING

Spring: the rambling briar and bramble,
Stagnant pool, a gaze fixed
Untroubled on the troubled sky;
Wind fetched what chance detached,
A sole plane leaf,
Witness of loss and no one's grief.

Winter: into that circle of water
A gold ring flicked
Slipped and sat in slime,
Thought of as derelict:
Thought of as beautiful
Light in the coldest depth of the pool.

They, the wayfarers, care nothing
For spring or winter either,
Their arms stretched like branches,
Tall trees loving each other;
But when the sun heaves
And fosters life in festering leaves,

And his long beams agitate
Over the pool of the ring,
Now they seem to need
Unhappening winter in spring,
Or now perhaps desire
The plane trees wet and buds on the briar.

THE PICTURE BOOK

Children climbing a statue:
But the sudden light falls!

Though the amateur eye
Swathes all shapes in a gauze,

Swiftly back in the past,
Precarious heron beside
A pool of spectral herons,
The soul sees what it was.
Like the dancer, aloft.
Serene, petals in sunshine,

Drooping, wilting, failing,
As if just at the thought
Of the last turns in the dance
Died the idea of the Rose.

When the shadow trembles
Purple and blue on the alcove
Spiral then up in the dome
Where none heard them before

Harmonies of the familiar
Ever and ever and growingly
Interwoven, chromatic
Till the ear holds them no more.

What? resumed with a sigh?
Though persisting so long
The soul's fervour prevails,

We are glad at the end
If the sudden light falls
When our happiness fails.

WAITING

We stopped and spoke as if no spade had laid
The final turf, no hand had taken care
With consecration of a patient art
To plant for us perpetual roses there.

Spell-bound, we walk unfalteringly on;
The stars grow purer, shadows blacker lie,
And yet we feel as if the dawn herself
Were wandering all night long deep in the sky.

SERIOUS OPERATION

Love of myself was deepest:
And though I suffered long,
After the dereliction,
After the heart's wrong,
Crueller than the knife the pain
Of knowing will remain.

The wish to die for ever
And the wish for life
In one bed grow together,
The moment of the knife
Persists, as if the lover were
The unknown murderer.

THE DISPOSSESSED

That was my people's home: there patiently
They looked for water under the bare sky.
I left them in the desert land,
I stumbled through an age of sun and sand.
That was their home: I saw the fruitless palm,
The exile's prayer, the lover's calm.

That was their home. But on this empty day
Who will be coming a long way
Beyond the barbed-wire, from the impartial blue,
To say: 'my son, what have they done to you?'
And if I can forget the face,
How can I say I know this place?

Yet tell my people, through the living gates
I see again the tree whose golden dates
Once showered into my hands, I fed and lived,
My patience worked that miracle of gift!
That was their home, I know it: so again
Say to my people, I remembered them.

THE OTHERS

Another, methodically I repeat, another
Manifestation of time's mastery,
The clogged throat, the forgotten pipe gone out,
The sneeze on emerging from shadow into sunlight—
Surely these things happened to another.

Also malaise and the flutter of a feather.
Such comic unhappiness did not happen before,
The picture reframed, the visitor's courteous denial
Rightly assigned: I saw her open the door,
But that was yesterday and we are not together.

One face is withdrawn to save the other,
Courtesy demanded and a whole tray of cups,
The game played by myself and conversation adjusted
By someone similar over tasteless tea;
He is like me: in blood I am his brother.

I will speak to her when we first gather
White flowers; I have waited for her before
And considered then the stranger's veil.
One spasm of the artery outlasts her infinite
And her eventless thoughts of a dead father.

Smilingly we turn and speak no further.
Having received that visit I must not
Weigh down her grave with too much thought of flowers.
She was a queen and would not raise her veil,
Beneath its mourning gauze ever another.

AFTER THE PARTY

That was a very different story.
The moon has forgotten the plane trees,
Sundial is lost in darkness,
The dead leaves and the dead bird covered;
Feather, seedling and bone
Drunk by the calm wind.

What are these wandering strands
Like silk floating in the air,
Exotic cigarette-smoke?
What is this crystal sojourn,
Echo, an oracle,
Or artificial fountain?
And this enchanted laughter,
Enchanted voice repeating
'That was a very different story'?

Turn away in the darkness,
Turn away from the sound of shuffling voices,
Say to those pygmy syncretists,
Circumscribers of man's dues and duties,
'I do not think you honour God.'

THE FIRE HUNT

First the wind
High, high, buffeting the chimney pots,
No rain, grey cloud, grey sky. Then the traffic hushed,
Flurry of the scurrying black dots.
Beside the ledge stood one in a black cloak
Poised there, assured, windswept; and then obscured
Behind a rolling cloud of smoke.

Then the wind blew, and the smoke shredded to nothingness.

The cloaked one gone.

Below, the hoarse blurred sound, the far-off grinding and crashing,
The current of the street flowed on.
Above, the chimney pots huddled together
Like gossips; still the wind, no drop of rain
On sea of chimney stacks. Movement among the gables,
A stir, the smoke-drift, and again
Smoke over stacks and gables, over fire-escapes. The wind
Still mounting, the cracked slate toppling, the air
Dry as it was in the beginning: and beginning there
(First formless) forming, rising higher,
The singing of the telegraph wire.

Then the wind blew, and the height was calmed and rainless.

And no rain came.

Then the laughter began, and feet in the rafter; the rustle became
Distincter, like dry leaves brushed into a flame,
And one touched the skylight, clawing and pawing and feeling
   for the ceiling,
One darted by the skylight: the lightless form
Grew formless, the mobile clouds concentred for the coming
   storm,
Reforming: each window bright with livid light.

Then the wind blew, and the silence was broken by voices.

And all throats dry.

Clamber up iron stairs, the hurry and outcry,
Feet on the parapet, the wire singing, the white light swinging
To and fro between the tottering gables.
From level of the ground
Moving, a swell of sound, the voices, separating, thinning. . . .
But then, as it was in the beginning,
The far-off voices whispering, growing, rising from
The confused mass, emerge and merge and swell.

Then the wind ceased, and the silence was of a great gentleness.

And God's rain fell.

THE SILVER TRAY

We who sustain, contain our race
Today, as in its being we see
Each star single and sole in space
Meaning a constellation: we

Live ever under the third sign,
Gemini—but unanimous
Only as in that silver design
The hunter and the hunted are thus.

Not this twin birth could make us one,
Nor any souls' first face-to-face,
Never the supreme unison:
Merely, we both perceived the chase.

Lost the hunt over the broken hills?
The contravention of 'I' and 'You'?
All lost, lost last concord of wills
When I remember, we were two.

What reigned between us when we were born?
If it was found, or could be found,
I found it at the cry of the horn,
I lost it at the bay of the hound.

If it was in our hearts before,
What remains now, eternal, there?
The chase: between us reigns no more
The silence at the flight of the hare.

BROTHERS

A cloud blows over,
Darkens the moon's face,
Thunder bursts over the chalet.
And downfall, downfall, downfall,
Into the black chasm
The oldest brother
Turned to a black stone, Schwarz!

And Hans, the other brother?
Amid the zizz of mosquitoes,
Tinkle of the cow-bells,
Imagined overtone
Of the convent bell
Five miles beneath,
A faint cry . . .
Down goes the other brother,
Turned to a black stone.

But Gluck, the young one, standing,
Hands filled with golden moss,
King of the golden river,
His eyes contain the dawn,
His heart a bell ringing the Resurrection.

MERE INTERLUDE

Feel the colour of the heather
Not seen in evening, but a living colour
Felt from the shadow of the fir tree
Rising in evening, in the grey weather

From the shadow of the fir tree, the lengthened shadow

And the hollow, the hollow breaking
With a deep rut the woodland line, dissolving
Far off in a fine mist, the woodland line
Involving with a vapour like breathing, wreathing
The woodland line with vapour

In the partridge cry and the small sound, surprise of evening, living
At the interlude between the rising and fall
Of sound and colour, and the call, if only
The wild ducks' grating, waiting
The ear to hear: and among the musical droppings, the smallest branches of the fir tree,
Nodules of gorse

Half-heard, in the purring of the night-jar
Clap of wings across the furze and bracken.
The poignancy of three wild ducks
Descent of the hoarse cry through the darkness
One partridge calling on a hill

And the rest still, and the dead music, repose of a pool
And on the near pool the clear sharp sound
The flock of swans in the night air had gathered there around

Had been, in the breathing night, the mere interlude
In the wild ducks' flight, the melancholy three,
Brought
By the dead livid pool, in the gorse breath was
Given: no skill to see, unseen
Had been, followed at intervals the hollows,
Stagnant: but over the night pond
Of swans, taken across,
Had been, in the partridge cry, the vast continuing wind, the
   stops and music of the night-jar,
Lost.

RENEWAL

Reeds in the lake turned golden,
And made night day;
Ten years had made my eyes less blind,
The place recalled a youthful thought to mind
That made night day.

The evening air would have to say the words
I feared to say,
The waters pray the prayer I could not pray,
The golden reeds become in make-believe
The people in a younger world than this
Who make night day.

TENEBRAE

1

Inability to recall my mother's face
Restores me to where I am:
(Composition of place.)
Immaculate but ill-lighted interior,
'Not what I believe, but what groups of people do',
The air both sweet and stale with former incense,
The click of beads, the black shawls, the roomy nuns.

2

The service of *Tenebrae*
When the candles are put out one by one.
Opportunity for traditional preachment
On other lights that go out one by one,
The faces of the dear dead;
The friends;
The books we have read;
These lights going out one by one.

3

But the last one
(Sermon will come affirmative there)
The last one is not put out:
It is hidden behind the altar.

No need to locate that symbol
In the great atlas of ritual?
But what is it for the traveller without maps?
A continuing witness:
Or an absent witness?

4

Can I be allowed—thinking of the last light—
A more metaphysical sense of the passing of life?
If I truly loved, if my love was clear and pure,
No longer a claim to ownership,
Am I already in that other world?
And the empirical tang and mutter around me,
Is it only an 'atmosphere',
Warmly, communally, comfortably covering
Currents from the deeper, vaster, ill-explored, the chilly vault?
Is what I see and feel like that small window
Through which comes now a hint of the Atlantic breath
Out of the radiant everlasting salt?

5

An ordinary sense of time's passing
(As stag voices bay the *Miserere*)
Makes me again one of the congregation,
The black shawls, the click of beads, the iron gentleness of nuns' faces.
'Not what I believe, but what groups of people do',
Groups of people moving,
Groups of people standing about,
One or two with their heads in their hands,
Rustle of feet, coughing,
Doors open and shut,
Withdrawal continuing.

6

I remain with the sense of life continuing,
And even the subtle presence of the dead
Is like the silence that surrounds a story
After the last page is read;
I always knew that story:
It satisfies me but it is not final.

THEMATIC APPERCEPTION

I asked the cuckoo: bring a green leaf, bring a golden leaf.

Under the golden leaf
I saw the old woman spinning her grey hair in a loom.

Under the green leaf
I saw the laughter, dancing, summer idyll in the dreary land,
Fiddlers, the merrymind, the dancing-floor.

Under the golden leaf
I saw the Lords of Castle White and Castle Grey
Digging for acorns, turn away with blank eyes from the boy and girl.

I saw the milk poured out, the wine poured out,
The great grey pigs grunting in the twilight.

And under the green leaf
I saw the hardhold and the drypenny cast off, the Lords let fall their spades
And stared like men awakened at the summer sky, their lands, their homes, their children.

II

THE PRETENDER

Strange twilight,
Tender light
Of an ambiguous hour.
Under a sad sky,
Out of cramped rooms
Full of heavy furniture,
Gruesome Victorian ornaments,
The gas-jets popping,
Bulkily into my time
His rubber-tipped stick thudding,
He pads, the Claimant,
In the strange twilight,
Gentle light
Of an equivocal hour.

And suppose I sponsor him?
Benignly answer him,
'The rights are yours, the place is yours,
'Take possession,
'Be me.'
Let him occupy the alcove and the closet,
Nook and cranny.
I should be one of many,
Relieved, believed, purged:
Sincere pretenders,
Actors even in sleep,
Believed, relieved

Permanently of the *other*,
The young and shining one,
Waving him away
In the twilight,
Strange twilight,
Milder light
Of absolute day.

AN AUTHOR

Here is your Prospect to transform,
The quince-shaped moon crumbles in storm,
And over the towers your enemies grin and fawn.

But he, the peasant's rage
At iron agents in a sallow age,
Grimaced amid the flitting storm, defended his printed page.

What he has said has been said since:
Of what advantage is the menacing prince?
His face like the moon's is the shape of quince,

His spindly legs frightened away the lady
When from his improbable embrace she woke,
Poor victim of the nose and cloak

Moon-quaked by her and heavy weather,
Two goggling notions protrude together;
He died screaming for an absurd ladder.

What I have said he has said first:
Our prospect is transformed, and that was curst,
The best corrupted is the worst.

The Government has awarded flowers:
Once he took shelter from the official trees in stormy hours;
Now his enemies have fled defeated from the towers.

MURDERERS OF MEMORY

Usually happy,
We keep the unique picture:
We do not want a copy

Safe from stains or rain's damage,
The face from the dark town
Made in the image

Of passion and precision,
Now mooning over the roof,
Mouth gaping in derision.

We fear that fear or fever
Which paralyses when we turn
Hanging up the receiver,

And see the ingratiating terror,
The unpredicted likeness
Smiling at us in the mirror.

A HERO

Such matronly moonlit endearments,
Such bright horizons for a mother's lust!
Tonight his real memories are dormant,
Amid tourbillions of golden dust
He is crowned, enters his laureate phase.

Trophies are not banal
To this conqueror who planned nothing.
Men find such loud appraisals necessary,
Drum, fife, trumpeter mouthing.
Flowers of ice, summer in January
Filigree-figured on window-panes.

Tonight his home-coming, then
A wreath upon his marble head, and
Then the public secrecy of caresses,
His face buried in white hair; then to bed and
Reassuring music—not a dream menaces.
Winter crosses the triumphant spring,

Pauses white-haired at dawn
A lady fluttering snowy garments,
Touches his bouquet, chills the frenzied flowers.
There will be no more maidenly endearments;
Frost chinks, drinking a glass of water. Hours
Are days, days years, years silent as he.

LOST LAUGHTER OF INFANCY

The old clock in the old clock-tower
Devours his spidery fingers.
Drinking heaven's juice those two
Platypus in their furry bower
Hang beaks into the blue.
Upon the down's brown edge their warm
Egg of silver lingers.
At noonday the shell breaks.
The famous husband and his rib
Across the garden stumbling
Escort their red-yolk-nourished boy,
Complacent tears are tumbling
Down his vast golden bib.

Bring out the tongs and tambourine,
The silent snake has no guitar
But baby beats a drum.
An eye of turquoise in the tree
Quizzes the avarice of toil,
Winks weakly at the sun.
Two admirable coolies thrum
On bellies full of sand.
Bring the tambourine and tongs.
Elaborately circumspect
His parents wash his feet with milk
(O sky whose blue saliva
Coils through his thin canals!)

Twang, twang on the umbrella silk,
His wails demand respect,
Polish his brutal middle till
His navel like a brazen star
Challenge the starlight of his eyes.
Only the tambourine strums on,
The silent snake has no guitar.

The ilex shutter's down,
King Penitence fumbles with his crown
And Satisfaction plays an ace.
The rapid bear of Iceland
Butts the egg-shell with his face.
An eyelash on a fur
Was dark detriment of her
Who sipped, the unruly noon.
A wobbling metal arm
Was the amusing husband's harm,
Who sipped, the unruly noon.
Telegony is wished,
Luminous indifference sucks a spoon,
Yesterday's band is hushed.
I built this bandstand with my hands
And it was my worst,
The bulging bear behaves and stands
Hesitant, fiery, as at first,
Now that the egg-shell's crushed.
Bring out the tongs and tambo,
And play the killer serenade.
Two celebrated gipsies
Roam the encampment no one made,
Eyelash and metal rattle.
The perroquet speaks harsh
Advice to their pink harlequin.
From a sullen meridian marsh

Sorrows insinuate within
Their moral nap at noon.
Bring out the tongs, bring out the clacking
Tongs and drape the wet night round him,
Feed him on slices of the moon.
This plump loved screamer in a bath
America mottled on his forehead
And veins of twisting rivers
Is not the apple of their eye.
He is their ancient apple's pip.
Then wife mix blood and milk,
Poise ruby drops upon his lip.
He jumped out of the silver shell.
Then husband water your sown seed,
Make spaces for the crimson plant
Nor kick the bloody root.
A stave! a fiddle! baby's drum!
Blow bugle, bid the big band come,
Taunt him with the vaunting tune,
Flaunt your fatherhood and flute!
Bring out the tongs and tambourine!
Make summer of the frost at noon!

MRS. BARBERON

The dead revel.
The buccinator muscle
Lets down two pasty shields.
During the long revel
Gay, placid, angry, only
Neither good nor evil
Only to be alone
In velvet or in silk
The temporal bone
Stiff and the near skin taut
Like skin on boiling milk
No palate prompt and wet
No hand to feel
Or touch: nor lips to kiss
Her loneliness
In realm of the unreal

Before the brazen candlesticks
A stir that flickers flame
That was a voice
Words and music that became
Loud in a concert room,
As words cried in a cup
Equivocally boom,
The flames blaze up
Now is the song low
The singer still untroubled

Only remembering
Coil of black hair, and hands
Filled with wood-sorrel, looks
Into the century,
A fate dark-stricken

Unsatisfied eyes
Burning within dry sockets
Ages of ages echo
The wailing ante-room
Remote and imageless
The blazing pond
Not to be gazed into.
Measurelessly beyond
The darkness moving on the darkness
The darkness blended
With the darkness
The revel ended

The latest loneliness
Knowing herself alone
Sickness without distress
Comedy of the bone
Rustic humour of the skeleton,
She is unmasked
There in the darkness
She knows it, knows herself
As neither good nor evil,
The one who laughs
The dead revel.

The Stranger
In darkness, and in darkness
A light among the seven lights
A day against the seven nights

In the darkness
The Stranger
In this place of urgency
In this place of candles
In a beam
Of daylight: in the *andante* of a dream
In the darkness
The Stranger
At flick of whip and harness noise
At close of day
When the hoofs clattered away
When not a breath stirred
When the small voice was heard
Cheerful, now that night had come
(A darkness moving on a darkness)
'Gee-up there, you damned old Chrysanthemum.'

III

MYSTERIARCH

No. The saint sighs, the reasoning python grins;
MYSTERIARCH upon the northern shore
Still coldly guards her brotherhood of signs:
The day of knowledge that has dawned before,

The smell of lions in the ancient night,
The Centaurs frightened of their memories,
Sobered by murder, pausing in their flight
Under the following shadow of Hercules.

Will she proclaim the second age of anger
In the great silence of the Consecration,
What she forbids, or lets the strange men be? . . .

We only know that when day breaks, the singer
Rebukes rebuke and sings in expectation
The green-topped privet and the almond tree.

THREE POEMS OF A PROPHETESS

1

Under the lamp the mystery of a name;
The pool of darkness: not a leaf stirring;
Why did I see
Anything? and (if I did see) what came?

A remote puzzled god, hater of women!
Nothing will happen but a falling star,
Says the face in the fire,
Nothing can happen but a falling star!

Must I never reply?
Charity, curiosity, my vindictive will
Pacified, and my lips are punished still?
My cloak is thrown about me listlessly.

Chance is my desire.
My benediction is a throw of dice!
My malediction is a throw of dice!
Oh fire that I become, oh lightless fire,

Is there no menace in that cloudy west?
By the viburnum, the wayfaring tree,
I bid him come
To rest his head on my mysterious breast!

2

Bare and moon-denying heaven
Fainter and austerer grows
Than the thought which comes to mind:
Absence like the moon's was given
To console me at the close:
Love's recesses so designed.

Did this body burn to know
Its transfiguration thus?
Did this torn embroidery clothe
Woman's pride so long ago
Chastened by what spoke to us
From the cloud that shadowed both?

Other women too were blest
With the love, but not the name;
As a bird this morning cries
Loud the triumph in my breast,
I assert him in the same
Proclamation of sunrise.

3

Taunt me no more as her,
The mad storm's worshipper
Who craves darkness and fraud:
I too am sick for light,
Fearing the wastes of night,
Fearing the thunder-cloud.

Suppose cambric and lace,
Studied or aimless grace,
A boy's love beguiled?
Suppose this was passion?
Why then your accusation
That my heart's defiled?

Jealous daughters of men!
Will you still hate me when
The lightning-flash has torn
The frowning night about me,
When I, lest he should doubt me,
Offer my youth to scorn?

PERPETUAL DANCERS

Perpetual dancers,
Why do you say no?
The gold is all lost,
The river is deep
Across which I go,
Yet once I confessed
Creation was sleep,
Perpetual dancers,
And to dream is to know!

You my first created
To whom I said this,
Self-forming, transforming
White shapes in the waters,
On treasure beach is
My gold of old burning
Among you, my daughters,
Perpetual dancers,
Why not say yes?

A SUPPLICATION

When the Panther shone,
Obedient to his brutal law
We knelt: but I alone
Knew and smiled at what we saw.

Tokens of the Sun and Moon,
Heaven and Earth that we forget,
Are we born too soon?
Our hands unclasp, our eyes are wet.

Conquered by the ancient dream,
I had hoped these many years
That we might redeem
The Untameable with tears.

NIGHT

... Night, great night,
With your calmest incantation
Soothe the troubled woman,
Help her end the starry fight.
    Night, great night,
With your power to console
Entering men's loveless dreams,
Bring the virgin priest
Tears that purify his soul.
    Night, great night,
On the road you keep
Which men call forgetfulness,
Send the banished son
To his home in sleep,
Then, then only, he will weep.
    Night, great night ...

DEFEAT: ORACULAR

Our contemporaries, desires
Of an evening, sentinel's
Censor flame of sword repels
From prospect of many spires

At the unkept rendezvous
While the rose and mallow sky
Fades above pinnacles, I
Have the night but not of you

The great starry mansion will
Stretch out into space and be
But my spine's desire and ill,

Under Andromeda the bones;
Manhood given the rhapsody,
Childhood the cold polished stones.

VICTORY

No constellations her allow
Who danced, who conquered Hercules,
More than a mass of roses now;
Him trophies and the memories

Of a great victory. But why
That victor staring, threatening,
Mocks the considerable sky,
His cry of glory stifling,

She can recall, who sprawls alone:
Vanquished the Bull, the Scorpion,
The woman victim? All the grace
Of grief that mimed or menaced her
Represents to the night no less
Than Hercules, than roses were.

FUNERAL OF A RELIGIOUS

Sombre September, rain
Dropping in pauses, faces
Along the brown leafy lane,
Suddenly sly faces
Hooded: neither man nor woman
Pressing onward: the hood
Made something inhuman
As human as it could.
Hooded faces rush
Like flames forward and rustling
Like leaves blown flameward brush
The brown earth lightly: hustling
Towards the streaked east
Towards glistening black skirts and shawls
Towards the damp, cassocked priest
On whom the task now falls.

FOUR PICTURES IN A GALLERY

I

The owl is perhaps the loneliest lover,
Skirling late, not answered by his mate,
Describing his orbit in the syke
As light as a bat's flight. He stares and declares himself, will wait
Silent awhile in gloom, then resume the primal moving,
Repair to tree-stump and prepare the tryst,
Sweep with white feather drift, with intermittent hooting,
Like the lonely ghost of a motorist.
This is the owl time. Are we tracing back
Mare's path at nightfall? The ghosts of those who thieve and reive,
Moss-troopers, cross our every path in syke and slack.
For when in the droop of light the autumn seems to ignite the bracken, and the fiery fronds are crackling
Under the hooves of the moss-troopers inciting their mares away,
During the skirl of the owl, you may hear them galloping
Reivers in early evening through the deepening reach of day, each on his galloway,
Fleeting, disappearing at moor and sky meeting.
And while they pass
There winks a little light among the dry growths, fleeting
Fire on the whin. Fire among the wisps of twitch-grass.
Fire in the dusk. Fire on the way. Beyond

The skirl of the owl and the sunset tinge of the pond
Fire on the way. Fire in the owl's night, fire in the bat's night,
An impulse burning in the wizened bracken-frond.

2

Serpent, cease then to lend your mesh of thoughts and knots,
And your fidelity which followed and divined her.
My thoughts will ornament this ruin, and her sin
Sometimes transform the woman to the serpent which will bind her.
Its weariness a theatre,
My spirit—not so pure that it is without idols—
Admires her infinite attempt;
Her body yields itself to certain agony,
And yet the grudging soul is freed—
But at once clasped by that engaging monster
Nursed in the blue
And twisting now before the gate of fire.
Capricious and prompt reptile, you appear
Amid the supreme tree, reluctant length
Impatient and yet languorous, a clear
Calm body like the woman's:
You lied, confident monster of black length.
Negligent beauty you perceived asleep,
You twain are doubly dreaming since,
And yet was my intelligence,
The cause alone of all these tears I weep,
More versatile and perfidious than you both.

3

A cloud expands across the violet sky
Deepening the twilight: and the ragged red
Leaves lie like blots of blood: in the trees overhead
The sun flaps like an impaled butterfly.
Beyond the roses and the poisonous tree
The garden darkens. At the garden's foot
Thick orange fungi under rusty bushes squat.
I need not tell you that an enemy
Lurks in this garden in the fading light.
You saw him in the covered lane tonight.
I have set down a blessing or a curse;
You fear your enemy and hate your fear,
Only because you hate him he is here:
He is your god and will be something worse.

4

I tried to explain the word 'justice'; everyone
Here can explain how I was wrong. I see a stage,
Painted birds, painted trees, a painted sun,
Parapets. Figures draw together, sway apart. Then one, standing alone,
Talks and talks, weeps, and turns away. He is as thin
As cardboard, he is cardboard. But I see the crowd that follows
Clench their fists, rage,
Jostle, jabber, cheer, become the audience, cry: let the play begin!
Against the black backcloth of the sky, never having known
That these were 'real' people, a puppet hangs on the gallows.

FRUIT

... Cool, half-opening globe,
Yielding from too much seed,
You are a world the Sun
Ripens, intoxicates.

If through the stiff gold skin
The reachable within
Bursts out in ruby juice,
You are the same, because
You are the world that was,
You are the Luminous ...

CARNIVAL

In masquerade
At corners of the street. The flow of drizzling gutters and the
  beat of sleet
On eaves on canals on bridges piers through stations
The patience of the crowd the unending flow of faces
Masque of the dead
Masque of the living and the dead, the dancers' tread, the flash
  of red,
Advance of faces, swirl and dance of faces in many livid places
The movement of the crowd

The light radiates about the boats, the image of the torch in the
  dank water sways and floats
The Man of the Crowd
Body clad in carnival, the circles of torches. Suddenly a cry
  remote,
The haze of light, one figure in a glory of crimson, stalwart and
  upright
The Man of the Crowd
Eddy and surge, the steady merge of many towards one point
The shadows, flying, start apart, are joined,
Bend, blend at black-fringed cloak; below, the iron banding, the
  barca still standing at an angle
The Man of the Crowd
The dot of light advancing, the midnight torches flickering and
  the dancing,

Vertigo under age-dark stonework by recesses, fury of the glittering eyes and the gay dresses!
The Man of the Crowd
The mighty shout, the uncertainty and the torches dashed out
Into the water. Silver-grey of east, cloudy fury of the wind-whipped sky
To sicken and to die
Green beams of the moon fleck the reflected sky

Under the balconies that overhang the street the thunder of feet.
One sang—
One stands above, remote, sardonic, many at his will, but still
Swirls his red cloak about him, scornful, mournful, waiting—
The rain patters the cobbles and the slating,
The light of dawn discovering these heavy hours, uncovering the domes and towers
The dances, the flashing glances, many smile but he is immobile—
The dance, in a thin rain beyond the watery river-lights,
Of Saturn and his Satellites.

Morning.
The crowd waits,
Every head moving, the mass motionless,
A gleam slanting upon the drooping slates;
Far off, above the sea of heads,
The gleaming arrow of light,
The crowd sways—
The doors open and shut, a knot compact and tight
Steers out, appears one man bare-necked, bare-headed,
In the midst, quiet, with one dangling arm—

For an instant dead calm—

Then swift, so swift, a rush through air that cannot flash
For one, flashing for many, lightning-like, long bright and narrow

In utter silence the down rush
The silver arrow

Light: and with its flight
A stir, perhaps a mere rustle, as though heard from a great height,
A thrill renewed through the still multitude
Suspense between the night and day—

A thrill like a poplar's stirring in the wind, the leaves shivering in the strong breeze—

Then the crowd melts away.

THE SIGNS AMONG US

The signs among us: all
The west a soon forged sword;
The flash of a star's fall;
The memory of my Lord;
Where he must depart
I know in my heart.

And when I am gathered
In a deep swathe of sleep,
I see the birds puff-feathered,
I see the earth none reap,
I see the clock's hand climb
Through stretches of black time.

What other man has sensed
Such equinox of might?
Or through the forest glimpsed
The stationary light,
Psyche, somnambulist
Wading through veils of mist?

These April lilacs dear,
This eye-rejoicing land,
Would hold and keep me here,
And half in doubt I stand;
Yet in my heart I know
Where I have to go!

SNOWS HAVE GONE: ARCHAIC

The snows have gone, the grasses return to the meadow,
The leaves return to the trees;
Earth becomes changeable once again, and the rivers
Flow shrinking past their banks.

Fearlessly now the Dancer leads her two beautiful sisters
Naked into the dance;
Yet the swift year and hungry time are warning
Nothing is stronger than death.

The frosts are thawed by the warm breath of the Wind-God;
Summer runs after spring,
But at summer's heels the fruit-bearer autumn is running,
And soon bleak winter comes back.

The moon may wane, and then she will wax again:
But we, when we go to the place
Where the Good Forefather is and the lords of the old kingdom,
We remain shadows and ash.

Which of us knows whether They will give him the next day,
The High Ones, as well as today?
Taste all your joy, so that when you are gone that joy
No greedy hand shall grasp.

When you have died, and the clear voice of the Judge
Has sounded out your doom,

Nothing, my dear one, will stand you in stead; not your breed,
    nor your power of language,
Not even your goodness of heart.

In the shadows remains the pure and noble Horseman,
The Chaste One cannot set him free;
Nor could the Hero break the chains of the man he loved:
Death was stronger than love.

PAVANE FOR GARCÉS

I bring you what was seen under the Moorish arch!
Not to salute its beauty with a solemn march
March of our lives so sombre, may beyond these walls
Anthem of them be death's or of memorials
Perennial, but this fountain's music destiny
Made to sway in repose sculptured the tracery
Lifting its frozen jet that bent to windward sprayed
The lingering Garcés become illustrious shade.
Oh balustrades and this balcony of a room
Graced of Infanta, laughing left the stranger tomb
To walk with grace the blue plains and has come and gone
Not to its dusty dooryard of the low Bayonne
Mountains beyond, what will be seen, what will be seen!
Let for that stranger grace guitar and tambourine
As if by chance the dance play in the memories
Not of another, absent from these Pyrenees;
What rose again will rise to hear the square again
Tremble with the far-off chanting of many men
Chanting the low slow measure ever on the verge
Of grief, grief without tears, these whitened walls the dirge
Echoing of the dead, dirge of the dead, the dead
This for a dirge have this, this courtyard to the tread
Of dancers' feet echoes what swells and dies away . . .
Let not my abstruse vigil of a darker day
(Darker than yours the day) darken the day at noon,
Or so for ever our sad theme the orange moon
Idle over our fountains, light the dancing-place

Of scarred sardonic faces and the women's lace
Lit by a star of genius would not need or heed,
Will be the theme: to cripples, hobbling feet that bleed,
Girls dark with light, supreme, will *be* the theme. Believe
As in a dream the theme, embroidery the sleeve,
Scarlet the sleeve, believe as once in a pavane's
Slow dance, threading the maze with bleeding feet, the dance,
What once was seen believed: believe that memory
This for a dirge has this, have been or seem to be
With genius ennobled and the star of it
At that dancing theophany the hard eyes lit
Of surly the dark watchers; when my life has been
A memory, it will be seen. It will be seen.
Oh fountain like this destiny, oh moon above,
Oh destiny, who live because I live and love?
Oh Moorish arch, for these am I to live, for these
Am I to leave this life its graver reveries?

MERCILESS RIDERS

Merciless riders,
Droning and drumming,
Do you carry the promise
Of my first coming?

Scraps of parched bone,
Hair-combings, nail-parings
Drunk by the calm wind,
Feathers and seedlings,

Are you the residue
Of problems and despair?
Grumbles of the crowd,
Mutterings in upper air,

Loud wings in the red west,—
Are these to be
Drums of time's cruel power,
Heralds of me?

WATER

So starry and pure
Water, that men in you
Taste their own corruption,
Fountain, clear fountain,
Break out of the cold years,
Reminder of release,
The temple of the blest,
Homes for the dispossessed,
The war, the peace.
Starry and pure water.

Moon vagabond and hardly
Moon, irradiate
A disordered life:
Music over water
Remote, imageless
As the blazing pond,
As the light beyond,
The life beyond,
Starry and pure water.

DOLDRUMS

Neither seen nor known.
Doldrums of the mind:
A navel-string uncut,
A great gate shut.

Neither seen nor known
In the mother's womb,
In the dark town,
Inscrutable pain
Till the light wane. . . .

But eyes are blind?
Oh in the best mind
What errors must be!

Neither seen nor known.
A breeze springing up
On the third day
Bears us to open sea.

PANTHER'S EYES

Eyes of the panther, meeting in the darkness
The vehement patience of a mother's eyes:
A nursing mother, her baby at the breast,
She prays for the brave light, which now has left the skies.

Prays endlessly for the order of love,
Prays that the winter reign, the king of thunder and empty air,
The cold permanence that sadly wheels above,
The silent rooms, the drums of war, the spire's prayer.

Tells the panther: freedom is your name.
Tells the panther: I am dark with light,
Blaze in the night sky, you different flame,
Bless me with tokens from the ancient night!

Panther, your mouth is wet still with my milk once drunk.
Shower on my bed roses from Paradise!
I press my breast for lips made hungry by the cruel air.
Send down that light, which now has left the skies!

REED

The reed in water says
I repeat the half-heard
Convolutions, harmony
Of my Lord's thoughts, the strange thing
He spoke in the dark to me.

You seem to rage, but I know
It is mockery-rage, my Lord
Mocks you, my friend,
I can laugh, yes laugh, although
I shake, my hair stands on end.

Raging or laughing,
The reed in the water says
Words in the rhythm of—the rhythm of
A dead mind, pulsing
At an impossible remove.

FOMES PECCATI

What the star saw
  By its own chill light,
  Obedience at night,
Evil, the fatal law,
Let the star tell:
  A woman, settling there
  The blond roll of her hair,
Knows that as well.

All she knows is certain:
  Though the wit and fangs
  Are his who overhangs
Her breast and drew the curtain,
Yet her null thought suborns
  His radiant strength to error;
  He stands before the mirror
Whom the star scorns.

LEGEND

Bestiaries lived; roared, bayed, yelled; the thicket spoke; the
  stream was a hound,
The royal hunter hunted by the wood
Ran, ran; shadows lurched; night stood
Over her kingdom and was crowned.

All that happened very long ago.
Now we have come to the memorial chapel,
Symbolic figures. What is that one? Calumny
Flapping, whispering of a dead king among worried people.

And these two represent his wife and son?
We recognize only on the graven stone
A weeping lover and a woman's prayer,

Accomplished: now the golden round shifts
To the boy's perjured brow. Her brow is golden there
And of gold too the curtain of hair she lifts.

RECEDING

Trackless silence only,
Not a footstep, not a friendly face;
Trackless and lonely
In the wilderness of time and space;
Blue smoke of receding caravans; black horses
Endlessly moving through the barren place
Pursuing their determined courses;

Not a cry remote;
Blue smoke of receding caravans;
Nobody stirs to halt them, or to follow
Vanishing smoke and dwindling caravans,
The groaning wagons of the Amber people
Into the lightless land of chance.

ATONEMENT

Red feathers in the sky,
The kingly power a child.
Grace of eternity
Accepted with a smile,

His science and his love,
And his TE IGITUR,
Acceptable above:
The sacrifice is sure,

Because from you alone,
Scarlet flames above,
Submission breathes, and none
Below dare say Enough!

The wounds of history
He healed them and forgot,
Suffers them absently,
Since he is lost in thought,

Not of the tortured shapes
Twisting in the blue air,
The people he escapes
By suffering for them there,

Only of what dull mood
His endless years may bring;
Desecration, solitude
Between white wing and wing.

ALANTRIS

The green of resolution withers:
Blood-dark midnight, falling blood
Darken the hoofed and hornéd wood:
The god is silent on the mountain;

Weep I must or sing I must,
But am sealed in sacred trust,
Dreamless silence, tongueless dust;

I dared not dance, I dared not sing,
And to meet the eye of lover
I trembled like a loveless thing;

And a banished soul I fled
Secretly through the blood-dark
And guarded wood; the world was dark,
Dark as if a god was dead.

WRESTLER

Though stormy silver climb
Above earth's rugged rim,
And for a little time
The wintry sunlight gleam
On the high ridges, I
Still live the night gone by.

Shoulder and arm and sinew
Aching, I cannot see
Dark conflict done, continue
In barbarous agony,
The anguish of a heart
Cloven by my counterpart.

Did I then fight alone?
Crazy soliloquy
That dialogue of bone?
I asked that patiently,
Trembling because I know
And knew what must be so!

IN MARCH

Will you be there
When the new-born
Warmth melts out
Tunes from Munchausen's horn?

Will you be there
In the morning light
For the newcomer
From rebellious night,

Amid hair-combings,
Nail-parings, or
Linen and silk
Rags thrown about the floor?

To press your breast
Will you be there,
For hungry lips
In the cruel air?

PANTHER

I know something of that feeling, I too have
Tied the spires together, harpooned the moon, intruded
In the void. (My joy is cursing.) Something of
That feeling, panther in me, pad-pad, puss-puss, a secluded

Purring, a pacing, pausing, springs and roars, and in the eyes
Calm: and in the pathos of the distance
Nothing, a calm day, a calm sky's
Thunderous phrase. The Forest never listens.

Panther in me I recognize tonight, a gleaming
Walk in a cage, the bars are in his eyes.
Look there, a shadow! flower! book! The naked source of
  dreaming,
Fly there, rest there. Only the Forest dies!

RECOVERY

Winter snow lets fall
Tears without grief.
Expiation
Is the child of joy.
In the light of the snow
Thoughts now can be gay
As dawn multiplied
In reflections below;
Now the night is fled,
The cold houses gone,
Weeping belongs to the dead;
There is the white boat,
The quayside and the swan.

DEMYTHOLOGIZING

Hands that held me safe in childhood
I snatch, for fear more horror should
Across the abounding river come
Or call out of the fabled wood.

The pathos of the struggling hands?
The prayed-for lightning in the skies?
The white bird's sudden flashing down?
The treasure beach between the thighs?

Their will be done: and yet I must
Stagger and stare across the brink;
Without a language now, I sink
Back into the tongueless dust.

METAMORPHOSES

Deep in the shadow was conceived
The radiance that I became;
Only the snake-misled believed
That my two natures were the same,
For when the sunbeam fell on me
New raised, too dazed with destiny
To know I should be One no more,
My soul from that angelic act
Shrank: the incestuous intellect
Mastered the monster that it bore.

My body's black and golden hide
Holds the dark fountain whence of old
Her thirst was never satisfied,
The long thirst for that stiffening gold
Black image which fell from the dark,
Curving above her obscene arc,
And drank and gave to drink, gripped tight,
Its will conception—yet too weak,
Though reared and forcing, could but seek
And find, not pierce, her intact night.

I shook because I felt her fierce
Death mounting in my nerves and veins
Dissolve my purpose into tears
Brittle and dazzling; then my reins

Burst almost; in the spirit beyond
I sobbed, a shower of metal blond
Hair loosened tumbling over my face,
And as the obvious angel woke,
The huge wave of voluptuousness
Within me seethed and rose and broke.

Possessed, my shoulder and its crest
Her cheek melted into; the strange
Flesh in the known flesh of my breast
Grew to consume essential change,
And yet these tender summits, this
Private abyss of wantonness,
Possessed, could recreate in me
(Black martyr of concupiscence)
Only that inward violence
Which was for her, virginity.

The world is vast by candlelight,
And was there ever heart so pure
That a dream could not lodge in it?
Upright, inimitable, sure,
Whatever you are, am I not
The first aurora of that thought
Of sweet complacency which dawns
Upon a soul that loves itself?
It is enough that in yourself
You see the world I lived in once!

Lilacs, farewell! the perfect lyre
Only exists to modulate;
Hereafter round my single fire
A million fires will constellate,
The palace change into the prison,
And dark clouds of regret be risen

In the first sky that was serene;
Dark metals, flesh and petals will
In dreams resemble: dreams, farewell,
I know the lilacs you have been.

Black witnesses of too much light,
Seek it no more, but weep, O eyes!
O tears whose first source is delight
So deep and deeper than the skies!
The vision of the brightest orb
Must feed on shadow; must absorb
The sad gaze it has met before;
My first love under my first heaven
Was all I saw: but, being given
The time to perish, I see more.

I see the plumed helm break, the bright
Shield shatter against the starry wall;
The world was vast by candlelight:
In memory the world is small!
Therefore should I confess to you
(Starlight of reason spears me through)
To you, my friend the enemy,
Through the night's lattice should I seek
Your ear, and would your courtesy
Stoop, bidding the armed angel speak?

O God! I can confess no crime
Save this, that I have hardly lived!
Impatient at the source of time
I immaturely reft your gift;
For as those sudden chords that ring
Through meditation's murmuring
Some truths are heard by all, but this

By me alone, that you alone
Have chosen to be only known
In absences and silences!

That this, the palest of all rays,
Paralyse night in marble: this
Idea a flying javelin blaze,
Or ominous comet! mysteries
And paradoxes wreathe your hall,
Yet these funereal garlands, all
Your mansion's majesty, O king,
But trouble a people you love not,
Who harden before idols mute
And dark without enlightening.

Ah well . . . I must console them then,
Mislead them as the snake, and play
A prelude to deluded men,
My instrument their memory,
The monologue of a pure flute
Returning their insensate thought
Ever to a departed joy,
Ensures that in a woman sunk
They still recall her milk once drunk,
Thirst for the source that I destroy!

They stare upon blue stigmata
Flashing like jewels in my skin,
They marvel at the dark and gay
Robe, they adore the breast within,
And touch, as if for amulets,
My throat that ceaselessly vibrates
Under its viperine ornaments,
Paying me honours in my sleep,
Their odious rites my negligence
Counts as a drowsy flock of sheep!

Be wise, be without oracles,
O human race, my worshippers!
Be mild, transforming miracles
Into caresses: universe
Of these caresses and these kisses,
This bliss wherein your serpent hisses,
Meet my cool eyes, humanity,
But beware questions, lest you make
Those waters, tranquil and opaque,
Lose their confused profundity.

You falter? Yes, the heavenly light
Is as the lightning, from that cloud
Threatening, outlining us the right
Moment, as when we cry aloud
Reflected in some clear cruel dream
As what we are and would not seem!
'It lightens! It will teach us!' ... No,
Through that torn sky will only shine
The loneliness of the Divine
That knows the thing we would not know!

Who will speak when I do not speak?
Whose echo will reply 'You lie'?
Islands of silence and heartbreak
At waking on the day that I
First weep that I was ever born!
Sonorous trumpet and sad horn,
What of the future? ... Twofold light,
Twain plumes of the dark flame that sway
And droop and mingle, one white day
When the two natures will unite!

Adventure in the future, law
Of chance, and rule of time: my loving

People, the human race, once saw
A spinner's moistened finger moving
And tracing the atrocious will,
It is predicted! they shall kneel
Before that Other whom I must
Call brother, though he shall be seen
My parody who lurks within
The sunbeam like a drift of dust . . .

Drunk with the empyrean? or
From sourer waters feverish?
They must be drugged, who bow before
The altar of his conquered flesh!
Honour to poison then: but O
Dishonour to him, for I know
His deep dishonour, know that he
Who scorned the angel that I was,
Within the carcase of an ass
Was hiding his divinity!